Speaking the same langu

Also available from CILT, the National Centre for Languages:

DIY techniques for language learners
María Fernández-Toro and Francis R. Jones

European Language Portfolio – Adult version

Language learning for work in a multilingual world
Ed Cherry Sewell

Adults learning languages
Eds Henrietta Harnisch and Pauline Swanton

CILT, the National Centre for Languages, seeks to support and develop multilingualism and intercultural competence among all sectors of the population in the UK.

CILT serves education, business and the wider community with:
- specialised and impartial information services;
- high quality advice and professional development;
- expert support for innovation and development;
- quality improvement in language skills and service provision.

CILT is a charitable trust, supported by the DfES and other Government departments throughout the UK.

Speaking the same language

A CILT guide to partnership practice in adult learning

Henriette Harnisch
& Pauline Swanton

The views expressed in this publication are the authors' and do not necessarily represent those of CILT, the National Centre for Languages.

The authors are most grateful for the support provided by a great number of colleagues in writing this book. In particular we would like to thank colleagues at CILT, the National Centre for Languages, without whose guidance, trust and encouragement this book would not have happened. Special thanks are also due to Nati Knight (Brasshouse Language Centre), Sue Grogan (Leicester City and Leicestershire Learning Partnership), Chris Ball (Cheshire Netword), Linda Parker (ALL) and Judith Haywood (Wolverhampton Adult Education Services) for their invaluable contributions and support in compiling the case studies.

We would also like to thank Professor Sir Geoff Hampton (Pro Vice Chancellor, Education Partnerships, University of Wolverhampton) and Professor Alison Halstead (Dean of Teaching and Learning, CELT, University of Wolverhampton) for their support and advice, which was much appreciated.

First published 2007 by CILT, the National Centre for Languages, 20 Bedfordbury, London WC2N 4LB.

ISBN 978-1-904243-65-6

A catalogue record for this book is available from the British Library.

Printed in Great Britain by Hobbs.

CILT Publications are available from: **Central Books**, 99 Wallis Rd, London E9 5LN. Tel: 0845 458 9910. Fax: 0845 458 9912.

Contents

Introduction

Why partnership?

Collaborative practice in support of language teaching and learning is not brand new; organisations including CILT have long sought to draw in a very wide range of stakeholders in other fields – not only practitioners but also those who influence all aspects of provision, from economic skills planning agencies, to headteachers, principals and curriculum planners. But collaboration is a very recent returnee to delivery in adult education. It is time to look again at how European, national, regional and local partnerships are created, what their potential is and how they work best. We take as our starting point the relatively recent proposals of Helena Kennedy's report in 1997 *Learning works: Widening participation in further education*. Kennedy's advocacy for collaboration as the way forward has been instrumental in generating wide-ranging partnerships of all kinds for the learning and skills sector.

Our premise is that partnership practice has the potential to make a difference, to offer solutions, to foster innovation and that it is much better than going it alone.

In her review of good practice of inter-agency collaboration Kathryn Tomlinson, quoting from other in-depth analysis of collaboration[1] on the impact on individuals involved in partnership or collaborative work, says:

> *'In addition, for individual professionals, working with people from other backgrounds can be rewarding and stimulating, as well as making one's own job easier by reducing the time spent solving problems.'*

She also points out the positive impact on agencies or partners involved:

> *'Benefits for the agencies concerned have been shown to include offering them a broader perspective and a better understanding of the issues, as well as improved interactions with and understanding of, other agencies.'*

---

[1] Atkinson et al. 2002: 92-113; Audit Commission. 1998: 29; Fletcher-Campbell. 1997: 59; Haynes et al. 1999: 123.

Language teaching and learning generally, and in the post-19 arena in particular, struggle to find their rightful place in the 21st century curriculum. Making the case for languages and making languages fit cannot be the objectives of a single organisation working in isolation.

Tomlinson warns, however, that:

> 'Not all partnerships lead to good practice, as they can be predatory rather than supportive.'

Partnership can seem very threatening. There is a challenge to autonomy in being asked to throw your hand in with other players. It is difficult to embrace co-operation when funding criteria dictate that the livelihood of organisations is still reliant on the number of quantifiable outcomes achieved as a single unit. However, examples show how working in partnership can support the transformation of policy aspirations into positive practice for the benefit of both learners and teachers.

Different kinds of partnerships

In *More than the sum: Partnerships for adult learning and skills* Kate Watter, drawing on the work of Derek Johnstone, identifies five types of partnership at work in the learning and skills sector. Research and case studies in this book confirm the existence in post-19 languages of these partnerships.

1. **Strategic alliance** is a key decision-making group that is essentially concerned with planning. Representation is generally composed of movers and shakers, the decision makers and senior managers within a range of organisations. The objective is to develop and implement learning through joined-up approaches. The Leicestershire and Leicester City Learning Partnership Languages Strategy Group is an example of a languages strategic alliance.

2. The **joint venture** is a partnership between two or more organisations that come together to develop and deliver programmes. Joint ventures can exist in their own right or sit beneath strategic alliances where they are the tool by which what has been strategically decided comes to fruition. Joint ventures are frequently time limited with a single objective. As part of the partnerships developed by the Black Country Pathfinder, for example, employers in the health care sector were brought together with language providers, both from the adult education and further education sectors, in order to

develop and deliver targeted community languages courses for the staff in the health care sector.

3. A **supply chain** is a partnership that forms when a lead person, a partnership or organisation sub-contracts work to others. This is a more formal relationship, frequently with financial implications or obligations. Within the European partnerships there is scope (and funding) for the creation of supply chains.

4. **Networks** are loose associations that provide a means of staying in touch, sharing information, debating and problem solving. The Cheshire Netword case study on p23 shows that with relatively modest budgets, yet a shared sense of purpose and vision, considerable change can be effected.

5. **Advisory groups** do exactly what the title implies. They offer advice to individuals, organisations and partnerships. They may be quite diverse in make-up including representation from a variety of stakeholders with interest in a particular theme or topic. Advisory groups do not make decisions but they can influence the decisions that are made. The Nuffield Language Inquiry was in essence an advisory group informing the subsequent decision to create and implement the National Languages Strategy.

Aims of the book

This book sets out to provide a 'rough guide' to partnership and collaboration. The case studies on the following pages illustrate that there is no single model of good practice but that all effective partnerships are characterised by a number of factors that can be replicated.

The practice of the partners in each case demonstrates the advantages that can accrue to the planning and delivery of language teaching and learning as a result of working together. They have accomplished creative solutions to a shared problem; innovatory teaching and learning; improvements in the quality and range of language programmes; imaginative developments; the pooling of expertise and experience; the sharing of resources, skills, knowledge and understanding; support for teachers and learners. So as well as showing how these partnerships work, we also take time to celebrate their achievements.

Target audience

This book is for those who are, have been or might yet be part of a partnership between providers of language learning and teaching for adults. It has something to offer to a variety of people: managers, planners, teachers, linguists, non-linguists, those with a general interest in languages or in collaborative partnership. All concerned, from leader to sub-contractee, can gain valuable insights from the experience of others. We offer information not instruction. It will be for the readers to decide whether partnership is relevant to them and, if so, whether they can see themselves as members of a partnership.

Our focus is on post-19 language teaching and learning. Although we make reference to examples of good practice in other sectors, our aim is to demonstrate the benefits that collaboration can bestow on the vulnerable world of adult education.

We describe the sector as post-19 because to divide adult education into narrowly defined contexts is not helpful. The services and institutions involved are numerous and a listing is bound to exclude some.

The messages about partnership illustrated by the case studies here are pertinent regardless of context since they are, by and large, general principles that apply to collaboration within and outside the world of education. In selecting the examples we have tried to show that, through the application of best practice, success stories abound even in the less than robust environment of state-funded learning. It is interesting to speculate whether the remarkable achievements of some of the case studies have arisen precisely because partnerships take place in a constantly changing environment. Certainly some individuals have been motivated to pursue and engage in collaboration because of the diversity and unstructured nature of the sector. There is a strong ethos still in adult education of commitment to the learner and to learning which makes for open-mindedness and a willingness to bypass organisational constraints in pursuit of the greater good.

What becomes clear, looking at the case studies that follow, is that working together can be challenging, stimulating and dynamic. It has the potential to either affirm or overturn practice. In services that are peopled with part-timers, partnership offers solidarity, combats isolation and promotes cohesion of thought and practice.

Local and regional partnerships

This first chapter of case studies focuses on four examples of collaborative approaches. As they are being described, different terms are used to illustrate key features. The reader will notice that there is a degree of inter-changeability of the terminology employed. Throughout the case studies we refer to collaborative practice, to partnership, to collaboration and networking. In the introductory chapter some effort has been made to differentiate between the terms. Our decision as to their choices was not arbitrary, but it would go beyond the remit of this book to analyse critically theoretical concepts. Because the terms are clearly not synonymous, we chose within specific case studies those that seemed best able to describe the inherent processes described.

The interrelation between operational and strategic partnerships is a feature of the case studies in this chapter. The intention here is to highlight key features of the work involved in the partnership process and the potential for replication. One reason for entering into partnership practice is to develop and implement new ways of working. The need for collaborative practice does not stop at the level of ideas and ideals; embedding the new and the novel often necessitates co-operative planning and delivery as well.

Post-19 education happens regionally in very different ways. Delivery is hardly ever consistently in the hands of one significant provider. More often than not a number of organisations and services operate in the field.

A key point to bear in mind here is that each partnership is unique because of the people involved and the context in which it takes place. Nevertheless, the process of partnership creation, management and delivery has features in common that will be illustrated throughout this book. It is not possible to determine a 'one-size-fits-all' model of language learning partnership. Where appropriate we will also include lessons learned in other contexts and attempt to adapt them to post-19 language learning.

The following case studies are chosen from a variety of settings and contexts, and together they represent a broad range of collaborative practice. They can be summarised under the following headings:

	Context	Driver	Funding
Case studies in Chapter 1			
Case study 1 The Leicestershire and Leicester City Learning Partnership (LLCLP)[2]	Local strategic and operational partnership	A perceived and actual common problem	Cocktail[3]
Case study 2 Black Country Pathfinder[4]	Part of national programme	Funding within nationally determined priorities and targets	DfES/Learning and Skills Council (LSC)
Case study 3 Cheshire Netword[5]	Adult education/Cheshire County Council	Innovation (ICT)	Lifelong Learning Partnership
Case study 4 Brasshouse Language Centre / University of Central England	Adult education/higher education	Existing partnership – Modern Foreign Languages (MFL)/English as a Foreign Language (EFL)	Higher Education Funding Council for England (HEFCE) and internal[6] resources from the two partners
Case studies in Chapter 2			
Case study 5 Learning Partnership RAOUL – Raising Awareness of the Use of Languages (for work)[7] European partners	(Voluntary organisations, adult education providers, community organisation and private language provider)	The needs and motivations for business language competence on a pan-European basis	Socrates[8] (Grundtvig[9])
Case study 6 ALLEGRO a Socrates Lingua 1 project[10]	European partners (higher education providers, national networks, voluntary organisation and adult education provider)	Engagement of disaffected and hard to reach learners	Socrates (Lingua)

[2] www.llclp.org.uk
[3] This is a term widely used to describe an approach to funding based on bringing together a variety of sources.
[4] www.bcsip.org/PATHFINDER
[5] www.cheshirenetword.org
[6] Internal resources here refer to both institutions providing developmental and revenue funds in order to conduct the pilot. Both providers recognise the strength of working in partnership and thus invest in the development of the collaboration.
[7] The case studies in chapter 3 are European collaborative projects. Aspects of European funding and relevant terminology are explained in the respective case studies.
[8] For more information about Socrates visit **http://ec.europa.eu/education/programmes/socrates/socrates_en.html**
[9] See note 7.
[10] See note 7.

In order to draw out commonalities and differences more readily, all case studies follow a similar format. They are described and analysed, where appropriate, according to a set of headings which are designed to highlight key elements within each case study. The headings under which the case studies are summarised include:

- Partners

- Funding

- Policy context

- Local context

- Outcomes

- Lifetime

- Follow-on

- Learning points

The first two headings are self-explanatory, as they list two of the key elements of collaborative partnerships which are: who is involved and who is paying for the work. The following two, designed to contextualise within national and local parameters, are aimed at pointing towards some of the driving factors behind each of the collaborative arrangements. The section on outcomes focuses on the raison d'être of the partnerships: what did they set out to achieve? Have these targets been met? Consequently, the final three headings aim at identifying whether the collaborative arrangements were terminated following completion of a particular project or, alternatively, where they were taken next.

case study 1

Case study 1

This case study focuses on a strategic steering group that brings together a range of strategic and advisory bodies, providers, funding and planning agencies and others. The aim of such a formal and strategic collaborative setup is to influence, shape and assure the future of the languages provision in an area. Key to the Strategy Group's approach is the alignment to other strategic priorities, such as regeneration, inward investment, post-16 participation in learning, to name but a few.

The Leicestershire and Leicester City Learning Partnership Languages Strategy Group

Partners

- Chair: The Leicestershire and Leicester City Learning Partnership.

- Provider representatives: higher education, further education, adult education, sixth form colleges, community schools, primary schools and complementary schools; the Centre for Deaf People; the Workers Educational Association.

- Other representatives: the lifelong learning departments of Leicestershire and Leicester City local authorities; CILT Comenius East Midlands and CILT Comenius Netword; the Regional Language Network East Midlands; the Leicestershire branch of the Association for Language Learning; the Leicestershire Economic Partnership; the Leicestershire Learning and Skills Council; the Chamber of Commerce.

Funding

- The Leicestershire Learning and Skills Council.

- 'Goodwill', i.e. time invested in the partnership with no expectation of financial gain.

- Project funding, for example from the European Social Fund, the Leicester Shire Economic Partnership.

Policy context

Formed in 2003 to assist local authorities (LAs) to respond, in their adult learning plans, to the post-19 initiatives of the National Languages Strategy.

Local context

- No strategic planning of language provision.

- Absence of data and information about the provision of languages in the area.

- A diverse and multi-lingual population.

- Good networking and support from agencies in the area (CILT Comenius, the National Institute for Adult and Continuing Education (NIACE), the Association for Language Learning (ALL)).

Outcomes

- A strategic plan for languages.

- Regular forums for sharing information, problem solving and planning.

- Improvement in levels of intelligence among providers and stakeholders about language learning and need in the area.

- Effective working partnerships which in turn have been able to release resources and enable innovation and development.

- Successful collaborative bidding for:

  - an audit of provision of language teaching and learning in Leicestershire;

  - an audit of the need for linguistic competence of small to medium-size enterprises in Leicestershire;

  - training for adult education teachers in embedding new technologies in the teaching and learning of languages;

  - the initiation of a resource base for lesser taught languages;

  - the development and implementation of a strategy for improving the offer of language learning to 14–19-year olds;

  - the development of a strategy to facilitate the accreditation of competences in community languages;

case study 1

- - the development and implementation of an extensive programme of training in skills for interpreting and translating;
  - the development of a strategy to develop training in languages for business.
- Close networking with other language initiatives to:
  - develop of a strategy to integrate interpreting and translating services in Leicestershire;
  - support of deaf teachers of British Sign Language through collaborative training and networking;
  - develop and deliver initial teacher training for potential teachers of community languages to adults;
  - hold an Association for Languages sponsored conference to raise awareness of the usefulness of languages with Key Stage 3 and 4 students;
  - establish an institution-wide language programme at the University of Leicester;
  - create links with teachers of language Learning to adults in Europe through participation in projects funding by the European Commission.

Lifetime

- Not time limited.
- Project funding dictates the length of some activity.

Follow-on

- Continued bidding for monies to support key activities of the strategic plan.
- Continued networking and collaborative operational work.

Learning points

How do partnerships begin? What elements of partnership practice are at work here? Partnerships do not just happen, so what creates the impetus? Some are formed around project work, some arise from the need to solve a common problem, some occur to pool expertise in pursuit of a common cause. In the instance of the Leicestershire and Leicester City Learning

case study 1

case study 1

Partnership's languages group the spur was a desire on the part of both local authorities in the area to make a joined up response in their three-year plans to a local Learning and Skills Council request for their intentions regarding the provision of languages for post-19 learners.

One of the most important activities early on in the process of partnership is to cement **relationships between partners** and to clearly identify the paths they might travel together. Buy-in to partnership practice is very important. People come together on the premise that they will only stay if they can clearly see what's in it for them. So from the first it is essential to identify what partners are expecting from the partnership and what they are prepared to invest in order to get it. It may also be advisable to map out the shortest route possible to the desired outcome to give a sense of achievability.

This process can be time consuming and requires strong social and professional skills. **Clear and regular lines of communication** must be maintained. Partnerships may well be composed of people who have been used to operating in competition and/or who have little knowledge or understanding of the sphere of operation of others in the partnership. Time and strategies for enabling people to come to an understanding of each other, of the context in which the partnership will operate and of the scope of activities that are within its grasp must be part of the start-up process.

Opportunism is a frequent feature of the early stages of partnership. Although the Leicestershire group came together initially around a relatively contained agenda, activists from the languages lobby in the area wasted no time in ensuring that meeting agendas ranged far more widely than was originally anticipated. This is an understandable reaction in a climate where chances to meet and work together have been minimal. In a sense, it is all part of the process of identifying the potential of partnership work, but a note of caution should be sounded. **A clear focus** on achievable outcomes must be maintained at all times to avoid partnerships becoming little more than talking shops. People must be convinced that tangible outcomes that will benefit them are feasible. It is this fact that will keep bringing them around the table.

The first meetings in Leicestershire were characterised by an airing of all conceivable issues to do with language learning. These included: poor take up from 14–19-year olds; lack of activity in business language training; a range of issues around maintaining and promoting quality; the need for improving support for deaf teachers of British Sign Language; insufficient initiatives to address community language provision; scarcity of teachers; qualifications for teachers of adults. The list was formidable but reflected much of what was being said on a national basis about the provision of language teaching and learning. The first task of the group was to **prioritise areas of work**. This process was conducted relatively informally but within guidance from the local Learning and Skills Council about local priorities and informed by the group's understanding of local, regional and national policies that were likely to impact on the nature of language provision. It was soon apparent that the priority list contained major pieces of work that were not achievable within the 'good will' basis of the partnership so far. Bidding for development and project monies became the first priority to underpin future actions.

A collaborative approach to the bidding process is an effective way of securing relationships between partnership members. **Working together** deepens understanding and encourages clear-mindedness about what individuals can contribute to joint working ventures. Bids that demonstrate effective partnership and networking practice are likely to appeal to sponsors more than those lodged by individuals or single organisations.

However, it should be noted that there is a danger that a bidding culture may lead to a series of disconnected and arbitrary activities. This is particularly the case with a curriculum area such as languages where there are limited sources of funding available. It is tempting to make activity fit funding so it becomes critical to establish the context in which bidding takes place and to ensure that the outcomes of project work will genuinely contribute to the long-term aspirations of the partnership. In this, Leicestershire and partnerships in general, benefit from **impartial brokerage**. The strength in the chairmanship of the Leicestershire group by the Leicestershire and Leicester City Learning Partnership lies in its objectivity. This enables an equitable approach during meetings and secures a clear focus for all activity. The partnership's lead in Leicester has challenged the languages group to be outward looking, realistic and innovative. It has been instrumental in moving partners towards active approaches to problem solving. In doing so it has also opened up new avenues by making links on behalf of the languages group within the Learning Partnership's own networks.

Leicestershire has been successful in securing significant amounts of money for a range of projects. All members of the existing partnership have benefited in some way from the funding that has been secured. The implementation of project work has created previously unthinkable alliances, has generated a further commitment to the goodwill factor and inspired new partners to join. **Positive images of partnership** work greatly improve the chances of longevity and enhance the reputations of individual members.

On a purely practical level the confidence that has been generated in Leicestershire by the success of the partnership to date has led to some very practical self-help among its members. Sharing of staff and resources, joint staff development activities, improved local networking are just a few of the benefits that accrue from being part of a partnership such as this.

Partnership practice contributes locally to raising awareness of the value of language competence; it forces languages into the limelight and prevents them from getting lost among the series of pressing agendas that each region and sub-region daily tackle.

case study 1

Case study 2

This case study follows the establishment of both strategic and operational collaborative arrangements in a sub-region. The focus on languages as a curriculum area was of equal weighting the focus on processes and structures within the changing landscape of 14–19 education and training. Examples highlighted in the case study refer to collaborative language learning provision designed to be replicated in other geographical, but also curriculum areas.

The Black Country Pathfinder – Networks for Excellence

Partners

A broad base of partners was created, with representation from all sectors of education and training, as well as strategic and operational key stakeholders linked to sub-regional planning, funding and delivery of education and training. These partners included, amongst many others:

- sub-regional Learning and Skills Council (LSC) (strategic leadership);
- Black Country School Improvement Partnership;
- University of Wolverhampton;
- sub-regional adult education providers;
- Black Country Training Group;
- sub-regional further education colleges;
- Specialist Schools and Academies Trust.

Funding

Funding was provided through Pathfinder status. The funding came to 50% from the DfES and to 50% from national LSC. The local LSC contributed further significant funding in order to maintain the leadership and transfer of the project into sustainable long-term strategies beyond the Pathfinder programme.

Policy context

Pathfinders were national pilot projects which were set up in order to design, develop and deliver innovative, new learning for 14–19-year old learners in England. All of the Pathfinders apart from one investigated big themes in education and training and trialled some solutions. Their investigations included: area-wide approaches to curriculum planning and delivery (Wolverhampton Pathfinder); e-learning solutions in rural contexts (Shropshire Pathfinder); a consortium-based approach to 14–19 curriculum (Kingsford Pathfinder) and multi-agency approaches in dispersed and rural communities (Cumbria Pathfinder).[11]

In contrast, the Black Country Pathfinder looked at a variety of these issues through one curriculum area, that area being languages. Focusing on generic challenges in education and training through languages allowed the partnership to identify very specific areas of need and develop tailored and relevant approaches to addressing those. Many of those solutions, however, are applicable to other curriculum areas and lessons therefore can be disseminated more generically.

Local context

The Black Country, although representing a considerable local identity, is in fact a sub-regional entity, its constituents being four unitary local authorities. Much has been achieved in terms of collaboration across the Black Country that goes beyond languages in particular and education in general. The Black Country Consortium, for example, is a strategic body with high-level representation from industry, local government, education and training and levers significant levels of funding into key areas of sub-regional regeneration, education and skills being a high priority. The Black Country LSC also strongly supports collaboration in an attempt to spread good practice, avoid the duplication of efforts and generally optimise the use of resources. The growing sub-regional identity, based on similar demographical and economic challenges, as well as its industrial and cultural heritage, provides the local context for collaboration in the Black Country.

Outcomes

Programmatically called Networks for Excellence, the Pathfinder set up a series of cross-sectoral and cross-phase networks which came together to form a suite of special interest groups. Enabled through the specific Pathfinder funding, some 110

case study 2

---

[11] A full overview of the national Pathfinder programme, including a comprehensive evaluation, as well as follow-on developments, can be found on the DfES website.

projects were conducted. The impact is tangible and quantifiable. Specific outcomes are associated with respective networks and the following list shows some examples.

- Development of alternative curriculum models for 14–19-year olds, as a result of which there are currently some 3,500 young learners who are engaged in business language learning.

- Development of models for employer engagement which address employers' needs, as well as those of schools.

- Development of language learning that links adult and school based learners, for example an e-mentoring programme.

- Creation of resources in a variety of media, but particularly exploring the potential of ICT.

- Continuing Professional Development (CPD) and training models that specifically address needs arising from the changes to national curriculum, as well as general trends in language teaching and learning.

- Teacher networks which bring together subject specific expertise from across the sectors. Driven by a shared sense of need and a shared determination to support their specific language, colleagues focus on self-chosen priorities, for example the creation of interactive whiteboard materials for French.

- Regional British Sign Language (BSL) network which creates training opportunities for BSL teachers based at regional Universities, Colleges of Further Education, Adult Education and, increasingly, schools. The network also collaboratively develops tailored training and teaching materials for use by the network.

- A regional centre for the assessment of new curriculum models which strategically addresses issues of standardisation, quality assurance, moderation, etc.

Lifetime and follow-on

Funding for the Pathfinder was, from the outset, limited to a lifetime of three years. Partners who had come together through the Pathfinder, however, were very clear early on that they were interested in forming partnerships that lasted beyond the initial pilot period. Therefore, crucial issues of sustainability and long-term collaboration became important early on.

In contrast to the case study on the Leicestershire Languages Learning Partnership, collaboration in the instance of the Black Country was driven by the funding available through the Pathfinder and a commonly identified area of need. Although fortuitous, and most definitely extremely welcome, the seed-corn funding through the 14–19 Pathfinder programme gave a particular focus to the collaborative activity. Given the history of resourcing language learning across the sectors, most significantly, of course, in the adult education context, the funding was a welcome catalyst to initiate developments.

The downside of collaboration driven by funding is obvious: without clear leadership, and in order to ensure broad representation across the sectors, collaboration could well lead to a scatter gun approach. Those more experienced in gaining funding, for example, could dominate the process which, in turn, would do nothing to secure strategic working. This danger was averted in the Black Country collaborative partnership not least by a very proactive and focused executive group, led by the local LSC.

Learning points

Two examples which particularly involved partnerships with adult education expertise illustrate both the potential for success, and some of the pitfalls that are worth bearing in mind for colleagues who may wish to replicate Network for Excellence's approach.

Example A: Cross-sectoral resource creation

As curriculum choices were being developed for students in Key Stage 4 and beyond, a need for high quality and motivating resources arose. True to the Pathfinder approach of facilitating networks based on specific expertise and specialism, teachers came together with complementary levels of expertise and experience. Colleagues with a background in adult education, and within that specifically with expertise in business language teaching, met with colleagues who taught school pupils at Key Stage 4 to form a creative partnership. The idea was that by pooling expertise and experience partners would contribute different aspects of the resources. The brief was to create resources designed to support school pupils at fourteen for an

case study 2

alternative, more business-oriented languages curriculum.

The newly formed partnership planned the resources as well as the action plan for the production process. To begin with, therefore, the group designed a project brief, outlining project outcomes, key aims and objectives, as well as timelines, allowing for design, piloting/testing and revision. A guiding principle here was the recognition of integrity and expertise within the partnership. The adult education tutors brought with them the knowledge and expertise of a business language curriculum. The school teachers, on the other hand, contributed a clear knowledge of the target audience and all aspects of school-based delivery. Throughout the process of resource creation, therefore, there was a continuous and reciprocal reality check. There were many potential pitfalls: some colleagues from schools who had been so used to teaching national curriculum, and nothing but, for many years were driven, almost subconsciously, by a teaching-to-test mentality. Given the climate of overall testing, of measuring success against performance targets, who could blame the teachers? Colleagues with the business language expertise in an adult education context, on the other hand, had a limited experience of the target group of learners and therefore benefited from the knowledge and professional expertise coming from the 14–19 teachers.

The respective gaps in expertise often lead to feelings of uncertainty and, in an effort to overcome those, to overcompensation through protectiveness and 'ghettoisation'. Some of the initial difficulties within this collaboration were clearly linked to fear of uncertainties and the pace of change. The introduction of an entitlement curriculum for languages in the upper secondary sector has led to dramatic changes in terms of numbers of young people learning languages. The group meeting round the table in this project was driven by one overriding aim: to develop resources that would allow the schools to offer alternative curriculum models and thus to recruit more young people into language courses. A distinct sense of vulnerability and threat emanated from teachers and their departments. This sometimes led to negativity, often a sense of uncertainty. Colleagues from adult education learned in turn just how much pressure colleagues in schools are under in terms of student motivation, behaviour, etc. They did, however, also discover newly emerging similarities: the pressure on teachers in adult education of meeting exactly learners' needs in terms of teaching and learning, as well as curriculum, lest they want to see their learners vote with their feet, is a force that schools teachers are discovering in their own contexts.

The collaboration in this project took different forms according to what stage had been reached. The project manager, a colleague from adult education, organised review meetings in which overall progress was assessed and queries addressed. In between these whole-group review meetings, the language specific sub-groups communicated largely virtually and exchanged updates on drafts and re-writes of the manuscripts. The feedback from the trialling school teachers was very detailed and helped the authors to adapt and amend as necessary. The relationship, by that point, was one characterised by mutual respect and trust – an essential ingredient in the partnership.

Key learning points

- Mutual respect and integrity.

- Complementary expertise and skills.

- Careful planning/testing/monitoring/revision and adaptation.

- Trust.

One of the more long-term outcomes of this collaboration is that there is now an enhanced level of joint curriculum planning noticeable, with providers focusing on the development of particular specialisms, as well as a joint approach to CPD of adult education and further education tutors.

Example B: Wolverhampton adult education into sixth form Japanese [12]

The City of Wolverhampton has been developing, for a number of years, a comprehensive framework for provider collaboration and learner progression. Nationally commended as leading practice, colleagues in the local authority have, in collaboration and consultation with all key stakeholders, implemented a city-wide framework for curriculum delivery encompassing these key areas:

- curriculum framework;

[12] This project was funded by a different Pathfinder programme, the City of Wolverhampton Pathfinder, but was closely relating to all language related projects within the Black Country.

case study 2

- underpinning systems;
- CARD (Choose a real deal);
- My I-plan[13].

These interrelated and interdependent strands have resulted in sustainable collaboration, based on a system of facilitating provision according to need, rather than providers providing learning individually. By aligning timetables across the city a huge variety of new curriculum opportunities can now be offered to learners. The initial collaboration started post-16, but increasingly this is widened to encompass 14–19.

The Adult Education Service in Wolverhampton is a pro-active provider in this area and offers opportunities to young people through its own classes. This means that on Wednesday afternoons, during city-wide enrichment time, a variety of language classes are advertised to schools so that sixth formers can enrol. Informal auditing of provision through the Pathfinder's adult education/further education group informed the planning of an additional range of languages and levels, offered to schools in the area.

In one example, a number of young people have now joined a Japanese class in which they are learning the language alongside the adult learners. Integrating such diverse learners as sixth form students and adult learners is not without its challenges. Will the adults feel intimidated by the young people? Or maybe the reverse will happen? And what about content and pace? Will adjustments have to be made? The collaboration came about by the Adult Education Service pro-actively offering a motivating and relevant curriculum in a language that individual schools would have found difficult to offer. The current pressure on languages in Key Stage 4 resulted in schools' openness for opportunities to promote language learning in general, and 'alternative' languages in particular.

In the event, the outcomes were very positive. From the feedback from adult and young learners, as well as curriculum managers, we know that with sensitivity and common sense a number of potential pitfalls were avoided. The young people, for example, were not used to working for extended periods of 90 or 120 minutes. When they therefore went into a break, the older

[13] CARD relates to the entitlement of each learner to an area-wide curriculum offer. This means that all providers offer their curriculum through an area-wide prospectus with collaboration manifesting itself in the planning of coherent progression routes (CARD). My I-plan is a tool that allows learners to plan and record their progression, as well as institutions to plan longitudinally, track achievement and forecast support needs, as well as attainment.

learners made the most of having a little catch-up time to clarify any queries from the lesson and get some dedicated tutor time.

When asked about what they thought about learning alongside adults, the young people said they felt they had to behave themselves, only to be told by an adult learner from the group: 'So did we!'

The feedback from both groups of learners clearly highlights the benefits of cross-generational learning. The young people in particular were highly motivated by the adults' commitment and understanding of the significance of their learning. As a result, the young people increased their willingness to learn, their commitment to the course and their ability to reflect on their learning. Through sharing the learning, the adults acted, almost inadvertently, as informal mentors to the young people. This will have impacted on more than just the subject-specific learning: skills like self-reflection, organising learning, relating to adults, planning learning and progression, etc were secondary, yet fundamentally important outcomes for the young people.

The adults, in turn, reflected on the opportunities open to young people due to the city-wide framework. As parents, some of the adult learners then took back the knowledge of curriculum opportunities to their children. This will have a very positive impact on the children's future curriculum choice. Including parents into the advice and guidance process through their own learning will ensure a closer connection between young people and their learning.

Key learning points

- Narrowing curriculum choices at schools/wide choice at adult education level.

- Develop specialism and then ways of sharing that/access.

- Mutual benefits of intergenerational learning.

- Enhancing of learning through informal mentoring.

This case-study shows that much is to be gained for adult education providers and practitioners by taking an overtly cross-sectoral approach. It cannot be underestimated, however, that the success of the collaboration here is supported, in no small measure, by the conducive framework for delivery, i.e. an

case study 2

approach to timetabling and curriculum planning that allows and furthers cross-sectoral delivery. Developments such as the area prospectus which has to be available in all local authorities from 2007 will support this process where existing arrangements still lack. This will prove crucial for adult education curriculum planners, as their offer will have to be made accessible for all learners in an area post-14.

Especially in the days of accelerated changes across languages in adult education, providers need to develop strategies which help them consolidate their provision, as well as break into new markets. The changes, in particular, in the pattern of provision in the compulsory sector evolving from the changes to the 14–19 curriculum, offer opportunities for specialist providers. Particular scope lies in the development of flexible programmes of vocational or lesser taught languages, the teaching of which might lie beyond the capacity of secondary schools. Adult education languages providers, with their diverse range of languages and progression routes, have a key part to play in this changing landscape.

Compared to the previous two, the following two case studies are very different in terms of their origin, scope and remit. Where the first two case studies are strategically placed collaborative partnerships, these two describe collaborative projects that originated from a commonly perceived sense of need and led, beyond the completion of the original project, to the establishment of a large and successful tutor support network across a region, in the first case, and a developing and evolving relationship between an adult education and a higher education provider in the second.

Case study 3

Case study 3 is not a strategic partnership, but essentially a collaborative project that impacts on strategic issues such as area-wide CPD for adult education language tutors. The case study shows an approach that is fundamentally driven from the bottom up through creating considerable economy of scale and a needs driven approach to finding solutions.

Cheshire Netword
Harnessing ICT to provide a collaborative virtual environment for adult education tutors

Partners

- A range of adult education providers in Cheshire.

- Network of individual tutors.

- An adult language learner as webmaster.

- One project coordinator (who herself is part-time tutor and curriculum manager).

Funding

Relatively small amounts of funding received from Cheshire County Council (through the Lifelong Learning Development Partnership), carried though, by the commitment and goodwill amongst adult education tutors in the area.

Policy context

Launched in 2001 in order to provide support to dispersed and very diverse, overwhelmingly part-time, workforce of language tutors in adult and further education in Cheshire.

Local context

Cheshire has seven colleges offering a wide variety of part-time language courses to adults and there are numerous providers in the region. The vast majority of tutors who make this level of provision possible work part-time – and opportunities for professional development are few and far between. For many, contact with other professionals is rare.

case study 3

Outcomes

The partnership has developed a website[14] which acts as a virtual staffroom. Through this virtual point of contact, teachers have opportunities to:

- share ideas and experiences;
- receive and offer peer support and collaboration;
- get easy access to information, whether local or regional;
- share teaching materials;
- experience ongoing professional development.

The site is a communication tool in three distinct dimensions:

- First the local element: an exchange of news and chat and sharing of experience between the tutors; regularly updated information on Cheshire adult language classes; news of local and regional developments are available. It puts like-minded tutors in touch and allows them to contribute their own ideas and share them with others through bulletin boards and email.

- Secondly, it includes ideas for classroom activities and resources and provides news of national developments in language teaching and learning. It offers carefully selected links to other sites concerned with adult language teaching in general, plus links to language-specific sites useful for teaching French, German, Italian, Spanish, Welsh and Greek. It thus encourages members to surf and search, seeking out resources and authentic materials directly from the originators, which gives a window on a wider world.

- Thirdly, the resource, if properly publicised and disseminated, allows tutors and other practitioners from beyond Cheshire to look in on Cheshire and contribute to members' discussions and resource bank and comment on the issues that we all share. Some of this publicity was disseminated regionally, in other cases a wider audience benefited from dissemination through DfES or CILT channels.

Lifetime

The project is ongoing and appears to be relatively low maintenance, as far as ongoing funding commitments go. It is therefore not envisaged that this project has a limited lifetime.

[14] www.cheshirenetword.org.uk

The website continues to be hosted and maintained on a small budget and continues to act as meeting point, CPD vehicle and professional communication tool.

Follow-on

Cheshire Netword is owned by the tutors who use it as a nerve centre, as a forum for exchanging ideas, information and inspiration. Already the site has attracted visits from colleagues from four continents, from Australia to Argentina, from Finland to South Korea. Closer to home, the Cheshire Network website as a concept has come to the notice of professionals in other areas of the country and in other educational sectors. Cheshire colleagues have therefore been asked to advise about the opportunities as well as pitfalls of building and launching such a website in order to help practitioners in other areas. Some of the pitfalls, for example, were an inconsistent level of ICT skills among practitioners and an ensuing need for training across a wide area of ICT-related questions. Other challenges included the need to constantly maintain a sense of momentum, which was absolutely vital in order to encourage a growing range of tutors to contribute and share the joint virtual space. Maintaining such a virtual work space is famously difficult in any blended or distance learning programme. A distance learning languages tutor from Finland put it very aptly when she recounted, at a Eurocall conference Besançon in 2000, her experience as the 'loneliness of the long distance tutor' – a feeling familiar to those concerned with keeping up the development of Cheshire Netword.

Colleagues crucially involved in Cheshire Netword have articulated a vision of a network of linked virtual staffrooms involving language tutors from across the country and beyond. They would see this network of websites all maintaining their discrete origins and the characteristics of their partner organisations, but being linked by a shared vision and desire to allow reciprocal access to these virtual staffrooms.

Learning points

- Collaboration does not always need large amounts of funding.

case study 3

case study 3

- A perceived need in common (Special Interest Group model).

- Role of technology in the facilitating of collaboration.

- Development of support mechanisms through technology.

Case study 4

This case study analyses the collaborative relationship between two providers that led to the joint development of a teacher training course aimed specifically at native speaker teachers. The unique characteristic of the collaboration here is that it originated from the fact that both providers shared individual members of staff. Given the diverse and often fragmented nature of the workforce in adult education this is a widely recognisable fact and could thus inform the replication of a collaborative partnership as described in the case study below.

University of Central England (UCE) Brasshouse Language Centre
A partnership for teacher training

Partners

- Brasshouse Language Centre (an adult education centre specialising in languages).

- University of Central England.

Funding

No external funding. All costs have been carried by both partners for this developmental project. Some commentary can be found further on in this case study on the implications of this.

Policy context

The two partners came together in order to strategically address quality assurance, including the requirement that all tutors, regardless of whether they are part-time or full-time, are required to have a teaching qualification at Further Education National Training Organisation (FENTO) level 4 by 2010.

Local context

As part of the Birmingham Adult Education Services (BAES), language tutors at Brasshouse Language Centre are able to draw on CPD and training offered through the BAES Staff Development Services. However, none of this training fully addresses language specific issues. Through the co-existence, however, of the English as a Foreign Language (EFL) department at Brasshouse, there was a link with EFL trainers and teachers who also taught and trained at the University of Central England. This potential for synergy lay at the heart of the collaboration that ensued.

Outcomes

21 Modern Foreign Languages (MFL) tutors trained at level 4 (Certificate of Education), delivered very much in a MFL context in the adult education sector.

Lifetime

Until 2010 in the first instance.

Follow-on and learning points

As has been discussed previously in this book, the process of partnership working has a number of key elements that are recognisable and discernable across contexts and areas. One such factor is the need for partners to be clear in their expectations and intended outcomes. In the context of this collaboration this meant that both partners articulated the 'what's in it for me?' factor. This is not a drive by one of the constituents to 'take over' or dominate the collaboration. Rather, it cements the foundations of the partnership and therefore impacts on the longevity and sustainability of collaborative working.

As the partnership develops the Brasshouse Language Centre is looking at UCE to become:

• a resource for recruiting quality assured tutors in areas where supply is difficult;

• a supplier of 'trainee' tutors who would be able to provide additional teaching, i.e. to struggling learners or at times when fully qualified/experienced tutors are not available for example on summer courses.

UCE is looking at Brasshouse to become:

• a 'route-to- market' for their courses: Brasshouse would be able to commit five to ten tutors per year at least until 2010;

• a teaching practice ground for their student/tutors.

This case study shows the potential for collaborative working which develops due to an existing relationship with partners who can add value by drawing on respective expertise and activity

case study 4

case study 4

beyond the immediate relationship. Based on shared staff, specialism in this case led to an incremental, almost sequential, approach.

• Personal relationships, based on shared and complementary expertise.

• Project-based developmental collaboration.

• Strategic organisational collaboration.

Need was initially identified based on a needs analysis amongst MFL tutors at Brasshouse, as well as anecdotal evidence from tutors from other institutions. As is well known to tutors and curriculum managers in the field, the problem with existing level 4 teaching qualifications such as the City and Guilds, is that they do not contain a curriculum specific (i.e. language relevant) element.

In addition, the fact that although most part-time tutors are educated to degree level and beyond, they do not necessarily have the language skills in English in order to fulfil the requirements of writing assignments and reports at the equivalent of a level 4 in English. They require a more tailored and adjusted approach, and significant levels of ongoing support. As a specialist provider of both MFL and EFL, Brasshouse has a total of some 170 tutors, predominantly part-time. Across the two sides of provision the total splits into 50 for EFL and 120 MFL. Large numbers of tutors are part-time, often with short-term contracts, as is the case for adult education providers across the country. This is a significant factor in the management of training and CPD.

The overwhelming majority of tutors is female and fits their work pattern around family and other commitments. Tutors, therefore, do not necessarily remain with the employer consistently over a number of years and the commitment to training activity, be that CPD or initial teacher training, is variable.

Although all EFL tutors are CELTA or DELTA[15] trained, not least because of the British Council quality mark requirements, those who were trained under the 'old' CELTA model need to be retrained, as the previous version does not translate into level 4 equivalence.

In the MFL section, most tutors are trained to City and Guilds

[15] CELTA and DELTA are the benchmark qualifications in English as a Foreign Language. The syllabus for the course (CELTA – Certificate in English Language Teaching for Adults; DELTA – Diploma in English Language Teaching for Adults) is laid down by Cambridge Examinations Syndicate, as are the external examinations and moderations.

Stage 1, with some having gone on to Stage 2. A small number of the MFL tutors have a PGCE qualification.

Brasshouse addressed MFL tutor training needs over the years as follows:

1 Training needs analysis

Needs identified by managers/subject leaders via: observations; needs analysis questionnaires; professional development plans and communication with learners and tutors; feedback consultation and advice and guidance sessions. Increasingly Brasshouse are working more effectively with data (specifically around retention and achievement) in order to inform the planning of training.

2 In-house training programme

As a result of the training needs analysis process, an annual training plan is developed for MFL tutors. This training plan is designed to address identified needs and curriculum developments, as well as local, regional and national policy changes that are likely to impact on patterns of provision.

During the academic year there is at least one training session per term. These sessions are either full-day Saturday events or twilight workshops, often a combination of both.

Against this background, a Language Teaching Methodology course in collaboration with Aston University was developed in 1995. This course consisted of twelve weeks of training, plus assignments and observations. The course was developed jointly by colleagues from Brasshouse and Aston University and also jointly certificated. A further step in the development was then a collaboration with CILT, which led to some changes to the content of the course, if not the format, and led to joint certification from Brasshouse, Aston and CILT. This course was met with great interest nationally and the natural next step would have been to accredit it through submitting it to FENTO. The changes in the sector, manifested not least by the changes for the National Training Organisations however, halted that process. The current model presented in this case study could potentially offer a replicable way forward which could be adopted by adult education providers in the UK.

For the 2005/06 cohort there was no cost to the tutor for the course. Its delivery was funded by UCE retrieving mainstream HEFCE funding attached to level 4 provision. Given that a large number of part-time tutors at Brasshouse, as in many other areas of the country, are native speakers and not necessarily British citizens, the requirement of three-year residency had to be met. What may appear like arbitrary detail is rather a fundamental point: many of what can be described as 'typical adult education language tutors' (inasmuch as they are foreign nationals) may not qualify for core HEFCE funding under the three-year residency rule. This has clear implications for the replicability of such collaborative working and needs to be addressed strategically and at national level if inherent blockages are to be removed.

There are, of course, other costs associated with this course. The developmental costs are therefore shared between Brasshouse and the University. One of the key costs is Assessment of Prior Learning (APL), which, due to the very varied and different backgrounds of individual tutors, is time-consuming and thus costly. Brasshouse and individual tutors share this on a 50:50 basis.

Another key element of the course is the ongoing mentoring of participants. There are three observations as part of the course and the participating tutors receive ongoing support. The costs (some £450 per participant) for these are currently carried by Brasshouse. Alternative funding routes are possible through UCE or Birmingham Adult Education Service (BAES) as the employer of all Brasshouse tutors.

Negotiations are currently underway to establish clear future funding streams. In order to arrive at the final funding package, the relationship with the University needs to be secured and questions such as a minimum annual commitment of tutors from Brasshouse must be addressed.

For the 2005/06 pilot Brasshouse carried the costs for mentoring and related support activities, such as mentor training costs (approximately £100 per mentor).

case study 4

European partnerships

Partnership does not have to be confined by national boundaries. It is alive, well and recognisable within Europe too. Language projects involving European partners have been developed and executed through European Commission funding strands such as Lingua and Grundtvig. Partnerships that work across cultures and in which the majority of partners are operating in a foreign language are bound to be a challenge. European project experience highlights the key role that communication and understanding have to play in the success of any partnership.

The case studies in this chapter draw on collaborative experiences from two European funding streams. The **Grundtvig** action seeks to improve the quality and European dimension of adult education in the broadest sense, and to make lifelong learning opportunities more widely available to Europe's citizens. It encompasses all modes of learning, whether this takes place in the 'formal' or 'non-formal' system of education for adults, or in more 'informal' ways such as autonomous learning, community learning or experiential learning. The part of Socrates that focuses on language learning is known as **Lingua**[16]. It aims to increase the diversity and quality of languages spoken across Europe through providing direct access to language learning opportunities. Projects under Lingua aim to encourage people to learn foreign languages and to help raise standards in language teaching and learning.

[16] In the new Lifelong Learning Programme, languages are part of the Transversal Programme. Languages (Key Activity 2) replaces the previous Lingua Action of Socrates II.

case study 5

Case study 5

The focus of the following case study is on what will motivate adults to learn language for use in work places.

Grundtvig 2 Learning Partnership
RAOUL – Raising Awareness of the Use of Languages (for work)

Partners

Coordinating partner:

- The UK (a local authority maintained adult education college in the East Midlands).

Other partners:

- Germany (Volkshochschule in South West Germany);
- Hungary (an English language teaching school);
- Italy (a voluntary organisation in Sicily);
- Norway (folkeuniversitetet near Trondheim);
- Turkey (a voluntary organisation, Ankara).

Funding

A Grundtvig 2 Learning Partnership funded through Socrates.

Policy context

Grundtvig 'seeks to enhance the quality, European dimension, availability and accessibility of lifelong learning through adult education in the broadest sense.' Grundtvig funding supports projects that have potential to 'generate innovation' and one of the priorities of the strand is the 'teaching and learning of foreign languages, regional and minority languages and the languages of migrants and ethnic minorities in adult education' (Socrates Call for Proposals 2005 documentation - European Commission).

In each of the partner countries colleagues were experiencing difficulties with selling the value of other language competence as a work place skill. Mindful of the desire in Europe to promote multi-lingualism, partners had reservations about the extent to which messages were reaching individual adults in their regions and countries. The Grundtvig partnership was seen as an opportunity to understand better what might engage new learners and, as part of this process, to gain an insight into the attitudes of employers to other language competence in their workforces.

Outcomes

- The content for a motivational tool designed to promote awareness of the benefits of other language competence for individuals. The target group is adults who are in work or seeking work and the tool comprises a distillation of incentives to learn that are common to all partners. It is, therefore, European with national variations.

- The creation and nurturing of a new European partnership group that may form the basis of ongoing collaborative activity around the teaching and learning of languages for adults.

- A better understanding of how learning for adults is configured in Europe, which encompasses consideration of what partners have in common and so what can be deemed 'European' as opposed to what is inextricably national, or pertinent only to one country.

Lifetime

From July 2005 to August 2008.

Follow-on

One of the key components of the partnership's work has been to cement relationships in order to create a robust group. The partnership views itself as a long-term option, not necessarily in its present shape, but in the fact that its agreed working practices and the responsibilities that members have assumed, lay down a solid and communicable foundation for future collaborative work. It is the intention of the partnership to seek follow-on funding in order to further develop initiatives that are a process outcome of the first phase of the project.

Learning points

It is critical to acknowledge that any activity that takes part in a European environment is held up by the fact that most partners are operating in a language that is not their own. The experience

case study 5

case study 5

of European work offers rich linguistic pickings and more than a few moments of hilarity as participants gain first hand insight into the difference between talking and **communicating one's meaning**.

To aid the process of partnership building, Grundtvig projects require that one partner assumes the role of coordinator. **The coordinator** of a Grundtvig group has a dual role: manager, with a vested interest in keeping the partnership going and partner, with a vested interest in the outcomes of the work that partnership undertakes. The coordinator must be able to separate out these two functions in a clinical manner. The art is in ensuring that advantage is not taken of the position of coordinator to unfairly or inappropriately promote or pursue a national perspective.

The **infrastructure** of this Grundtvig partnership has both formal and informal aspects. Partners have entered into a formal relationship with the European Commission, with their national agencies and with each other based on financial investment. Formal bidding arrangements, contracts, common documents and processes for accountability mark that relationship. In addition, partners have informally agreed to a set of **rules and regulations** for collaborative practice that they will abide by in order to execute the work. These encompass use of language inside and outside meetings (does it always have to be English?); conduct of meetings; setting and meeting deadlines; the allocation of project work; communication channels and activity; roles and responsibilities. This combination, agreed early on, means that partners can confidently get on with the work in a defined and mutually understood context.

European partners, like any others, come with their own agendas. The 'what's in it for me factor' is as important here as anywhere. Whilst much of the activity is defined through the bid process and subsequent contractual arrangements there is still scope for people to try to bend project work to suit their own national, even local ends. European partnership work is **work at a distance**. Most partnerships work on a model of three meetings per academic year, each meeting lasting two or three days. This intensive face-to-face element has pros and cons. Isolating the partnership for a period of focused activity can move the work on apace. It also helps the bonding mechanism;

you get to know people much better, much faster. On the other hand there is plenty of scope in the three-month gaps between meetings for people to forget what they had said they would do, be distracted by all the other parts of their busy work and life schedules. To overcome this, good planning, realistic target setting and strong communication practice are essential.

Some of the complexities involved in working within European partnerships are further examined in the following example.

Case study 6

The case study below focuses on the engagement of non-participant learners, in particular from areas or groups perceived to be at a disadvantage.

ALLEGRO
A Socrates Lingua 1 project

Partners

- A UK and a Spanish university (the UK was the coordinating partner).
- A French national network of language learning centres.
- A national institute of adult education (Slovenia).
- A sheltered workshop in Germany.

Funding

From the European Commission – a Socrates Lingua 1 project.

Policy context

The ALLEGRO Project was funded by the European Commission to promote language learning to people marginalised by social and economic disadvantage, lack of educational opportunity, or physical or learning disability.

Outcomes

In each country the ALLEGRO partners set out to find agencies and institutions with whom they could work to widen participation in language learning. For the majority this meant going into new fields, mostly in the area of social and community work, and operating in a new working culture. They were required to:

- promote language learning to key people within social care institutions;
- persuade them that it might be worth giving their clients a chance to experience learning another language;
- learn the best ways to approach and work with the clients concerned;
- organise the language learning activities.

Lifetime

From 2002 to 2005.

Learning points

Each partner in the ALLEGRO team was required to broker further partnerships in their own countries and regions and to work with agencies in the social sector (for example charities, national and local services and authorities, the church, penal institutions) on initiatives to promote language learning to their client groups. The majority of activities – sub-projects - took place in community locations, outside educational institutions.

In each sub-project other 'micro'-partnerships were then required – language teachers working with social and community workers, specialist educators and staff in the collaborating agencies.

At times there were 'cultural' clashes: in education, for example, things get planned and executed to fairly tight and rigid timetables, whereas in the field of social care there appeared to be more fluidity, and this sometimes led to frustrations on both sides. It was necessary to both recognise and **accept differences**, to try to understand the culture and the systems within the collaborating agency and to go with it rather than try to impose our own.

The **prior experience** of the main project team was varied – some had worked on numerous projects before, for others it was the very first time they had taken part. They had very different reasons for being involved, not all of them in any way related to a passion for the aims of the project itself. To weld together a group of this kind sets a difficult goal for the project leaders. In the ALLEGRO project a combination of strategies was used in an attempt to create **project identity and team coherence**.

- Shared understanding of the rationale of the project: this is something that takes time to achieve, especially when there are different cultural expectations and understanding within the partnership. In the ALLEGRO project there were a number of fundamentals where shared understanding needed to be established: what is it to be 'disadvantaged'? Does this vary from one country to another? What does 'promoting' languages actually mean? What kinds of

case study 6

language learning opportunities are suitable for such groups? To reach a point where a project ethos is shared among all partners strategies must be planned in from the outset. In the ALLEGRO project these included allowing time at project meetings for full discussion of the issues and clear and unequivocal guidance from the project leaders on aspects which could not be compromised, while allowing flexibility in some areas which were not fundamental to the success of the project. Incidents that threaten the partnership are bound to occur from time to time. In this case much time was spent on arriving at common agreement about 'outreach activities'; in the minds of the project leaders this clearly meant that activities should take place in the community, not in the institution of the partners concerned. Some partners were very reluctant to accept this: they saw outreach as reaching out into disadvantaged communities but providing learning experiences which took place within their institutions. The problem was partly solved by allowing those partners who genuinely felt that encouraging the groups they worked with to come into their institutions was breaking barriers to participation, to offer activities which involved both working in community venues and opening the doors of their institutions.

- Opportunities to share success and failure: the ALLEGRO partnership recognised that not everything that it set out to achieve would be a success. Every partner had a chance to share their failures as well as celebrate their successes and tried to use failure constructively, learning from the experience to strengthen the work of the team as a whole.

- Open communication channels: an interactive email distribution list[17] was used to maintain regular contact, post information and exchange news between members of the project team.

- Visits: project leaders or evaluators have visited each partner. This has built personal relationships and enabled each partner to be the sole focus of attention at least once during the lifetime of the project.

[17] Hosted by jiscmail www.jiscmail.ac.uk.

Process of partnerships

In the preceding two chapters which focused on a variety of local, regional and European partnerships you will have seen just what breadth and variety there is in collaborative ways of working, and found some concrete insights and pointers towards potential replication in your own institution. In the following chapter we attempt to draw out some of those pointers in a more generic manner, highlighting therefore what appears to be common between the different forms of partnership working. However varied the case studies, however disparate the outcomes, there are common characteristics in both process and mechanics of partnership working.

What do the case studies tell us about partnership?

They make clear that there is a process involved which includes four stages:

- **Initiation:** people are drawn together around a concept, idea, theme, issue.

- **Consolidation:** the partnership is created; working practices are determined.

- **Production:** the partnership yields outcomes.

- **Evaluation:** a period of reflection and action planning.

A number of factors impact on this process and need to be taken into account. They include:

- **Time**

- **Money.**

David Hargreaves, when talking about collaboration in the 14–19 sector, acknowledges that partnership working arises as a response to the increasing fragmentation of the educational system. He is quoted as describing collaborations and partnerships as 'horizontal relationships' which 'provide a valued replacement for the declining vertical control system of, for example LEAs'.[18]

Although fragmentation and lack of overall control are features of post-19 learning provision, they are not the spur for the partnerships described here. Essentially the rationale behind the case study partnerships is the pooling of resources to solve problems in language teaching and learning that are beyond the capabilities of single institutions and services. They have grown from grass roots level in response to a variety of issues. Some have developed into forums for strategic planning but on a regional basis only.

There is a risk that partnership practice of this sort will contribute to fragmentation on a local level. Those seeking to model new partnerships would do well to first research what already exists. It may be that local partnerships, particularly those that embrace learning, will provide a ready-made framework for developments in languages teaching and learning.

The four stages of the partnership process

The case studies show us that the **initiation** part of the partnership process can be either planned or spontaneous. European projects begin with the concept of partnership. Bringing people together is as important as the language outcomes that ensue. Cheshire Netword, on the other hand, arose from a single issue (the support of part-time teaching staff) and partnership became the chosen tool to address the problem.

It is important to recognise that partnership is not an end in itself. It is the means by which other things happen. Partnerships have to be carefully designed and nurtured, but over-investment in the process of partnership will undermine their ultimate success. Partnership is not straightforward, not easy and not part of the culture of every organisation, region and individual. In an analysis of the 14–19 phase of learning, and the place of collaboration within it, Jacky Lumby and Nick Foskett write:

> *Post-1979, and more strongly post-1988, any culture of partnership was strongly compromised by marketisation, competition and central accountability and control. ... the dominant relationships were competitive, transactional or accountability based.*[19]

The legacy of this period is still with us and, as a result, it can take considerable time and effort to create an effective partnership and sustain it.

---

[18] Hargreaves, D. 2003
[19] Lumby, J. and Foskett, N. 2005: 138.

Part of the process is to demonstrate early on the practical outcomes that partners can expect to accrue as a result of their commitment. The management of collaborative practice and the achievement of partnership outcomes are simultaneous activities.

Consolidation involves cementing relationships between partners and clearly identifying the paths they might travel together. Buy-in to partnership practice is very important. People come together on the premise that they will only stay if they can clearly see what is in it for them. So from the first it is essential to identify what partners are expecting from the partnership and what they are prepared to invest in order to get it. It may also be advisable to map out the shortest route possible to the desired outcome to give a sense of achievability.

Clear and regular lines of communication must be maintained. Time and strategies for enabling people to come to an understanding of each other, of the context in which the partnership will operate and of the scope of activities that are within its grasp are all essential.

A successful partnership is one where leadership and infrastructure enable impartial consideration of everyone's priorities, assessment of individual needs and expectations and integration of single wish lists into a partnership whole.

Time and **money** are consistent features of the **production** period of the partnership process. The case studies demonstrate that partnership can be both the means by which money allocated to an initiative is spent and a vehicle for securing money to spend on initiatives. Both of these functions mean that partners will be operating within clearly defined time limits. The case study partnerships are generally focused on achieving the pre-determined outcomes of a project. To form a new partnership and meet a project specification within a limited period can be a tall order. For adult educators additional hazards are conditions of service (often part-time) and the context in which they operate (voluntarily or within turbulent funding). Partnerships like in the Black Country or the Leicestershire and Leicester City Learning Partnership examples are responsive to the demands of a number of different projects, funded from a variety of sources at the same time. The infrastructures of partnerships like these are intricate in order to service the complexity of the work. Accordingly, one of the key challenges to collaborative arrangements that grow out of these circumstances is the volatility of funding sources and the changeability of different partners' agendas.

Single issue partnerships like RAOUL will be more straightforward and involve fewer people. Growth from a single issue partnership is common and the profile of the partnership will need to develop accordingly to accommodate growth.

The possibility of accessing money is a strong motivational factor for partnership. This is particularly the case within adult education and especially for curriculum areas like languages where funding from mainstream sources, the Learning and Skills Council, for example, is never sufficient to meet all the potential needs of all the potential learners.

Evaluation and **action planning** should be ongoing within partnerships. It is unlikely that a partnership of any sort will exist indefinitely in post-19 education. In this sector partnerships are not about creating permanent structures for delivery, they are dynamic alliances that come together to address particular needs and issues. They are clearly focused on making effective working connections between organisations and are not about usurping roles and responsibilities in respect of delivery. As such, once relationships have been brokered and become the norm the role of the partnership may be changed or the partnership may be terminated. As part of the partnerships developed by the Black Country Pathfinder, for example, employers in the health care sector were brought together with language providers, both from the adult education and further education sectors, in order to develop and deliver targeted community languages courses for the staff in the health care sector. The initial umbrella partnership of the Pathfinder acted as facilitator and broker. Once the joint development had taken place, i.e. the discussions about the curriculum, the involvement of expertise from both the vocational sector and the language specialists, and the approach piloted, the arrangement effectively became a joint venture inasmuch as the NHS trust became a purchaser of (language) services from the provider. This is a relatively common pattern but one that is vulnerable in the face of changing demand. As is often the case with languages, as well as other training courses, when employers experience some budgetary pressure, the training will be one of the first expenditures deemed dispensable.

Other factors impacting on partnership are examined in greater detail in the following chapter.

Tools for partnership

In the previous chapter we looked at the process of partnership. Here we consider some elusive factors at work within partnerships that need acknowledging and accommodating:

*   the context in which the partnership operates;

*   the motivations of the partners;

*   differing levels of commitment to the concept and to the practice.

We also described aspects that are common to successful partnerships:

*   leadership;

*   partners with a range of complementary skills;

*   sound business practice;

*   clear lines of communication;

*   realistic, achievable goals.

Getting a partnership up and running will involve participants in deciding their response to these fundamental needs. Partnership infrastructure is important in the drive to build effective working practice.

The Opening the Door to Language Learning project drew out some recommendations for cooperating with others. The key findings of this international project group were:

*   Find partners with skills, expertise and facilities to complement your own and offer them something in return.

*   Do not work with too many partners.

*   Liaise with a particular person rather than an organisation and keep in regular contact.

*   Set clear goals and an exact timetable to avoid misunderstandings.

There is also a pertinent inventory of barriers to co-operation:

- bureaucratic obstacles (form filling, approval by committee, etc);

- partners withdrawing from the programme at the last minute (a formal contract may prevent this problem);

- lack of awareness and co-operation between departments within the same organisation (could also be a benefit if co-operation resolves this);

- competition between organisations.

What supports partnership working?

Partnerships do not operate in a **context** that is conducive to success. People are asked to work together to solve problems but within funding strategies that require accountability from single organisations. It takes a strong alliance to overcome the fact that the basis for provision – the funding – is still predicated on competition. There is rarely money to support making partnerships work, neither has there been training to ensure that they do. Consequently, a partnership may invest too heavily in its infrastructure, diverting resources and people from the work that it has been formed to achieve. It may not invest at all in the infrastructure, trusting individuals to make it up as they go along. There may be insufficient investment and a partial requirement of partners to work within the framework but plenty of scope for them to diverge.

Adult education is prone to change. Timescales are fore shortened by alterations in policy, funding, organisations or all three. There is little opportunity to build lasting solutions. Partnerships operating in this environment must work within the rhythms of the sector and acknowledge that the context will impose additional pressures of time and on personnel. A partnership that has a robust framework is more likely to withstand the unexpected and be able to change, if necessary. The framework frees those involved to concentrate on the task in hand.

Motivation

Motivation is a significant driver in the creation and subsequent story of partnership. The reasons why partnerships come together are not always as high-minded as we might like to believe. Self-interest, financial gain, getting out of a fix are just as likely to be motivating factors for partners as commitment to a cause, passion for a subject or intellectual challenge. Understanding potential partners' motives for engagement is important because, as broker, a partnership leader may need to appeal to one or other motivation in order to get people on board. In the same way as adult courses are constructed against certain enticing agendas, so the partnership may wish to make advances to new members through exploiting what is perceived to be their Achilles heel.

Once formed, the partnership will only thrive if partners are motivated to carry on. A number of factors may contribute to this. The assurance that individual partner agendas will be met – the 'what's in it for me?' factor; quick gains – smart target setting leading to early success; equitable management - all partners benefit from being part of the whole; financial reward accrued from partnership practice; enthusiasm and optimism; confidence in the partnership as a way of adding value to the day job or the home organisation; these are all powerful reasons to hang on in there.

The motivations and drivers for collaboration will inform the response that the partnership makes in pursuit of its common goal. Although this sounds precariously like stating the very obvious, it is worth highlighting that there is no right or wrong answer in this context. If the consensus, following an analysis of all partners' motivations, is that there is a need for a virtual network, or the development of a particular resource, or the collaborative response to particular training needs, then this is legitimate.

A useful exercise for any new partnership is to apply techniques for effective goal-setting affirmations for individuals, adapted from Ian Gilbert's book on motivation in the classroom, in an organisational context. Gilbert cites the three Ps of effective goal-setting affirmations – personal, present tense and positive – as key to articulating, in our case, the vision for collaboration. Where is it that you, on behalf of your organisation and in the context of this collaborative project, want to be in a couple of years? Start with 'I am' or 'We are…':

> *'We are offering the most effective CPD for our part-time language teaching staff.'*

> *'We provide a coordinated area-based curriculum for our city's learners.'*

> *'All our community language courses use tailored ICT based teaching resources.'*

As Gilbert suggests in his book, by then conducting a follow-on exercise which asks the participants to describe the route to achieving the overarching goal, or vision, it becomes even more powerful: 'To get there we got …'

This process also moves the conceptual phase of early collaboration into the next stage, which is to set out clearly the objectives. Whilst continuing to bear in mind the agenda brought to the table by individual partners, the process can now be moved into identifying the milestones needed to make a reality of the big vision. Setting out a series of achievable and measurable objectives also provides a useful mechanism for future reality checks.

Commitment

Our case studies show us that **commitment** is a significant factor within partnership practice. Commitment makes a number of demands on individuals as well as the partnership as a whole. Partners can anticipate that their own agendas will be considered and, to a certain extent met, but they must also acknowledge the right of the partnership to set its own goals as a cooperative. Partners should aspire to a common vision. The question that they need to ask of each other and of themselves is: 'What is it that we want to achieve together?' The answer ought to lead to an understanding of where the project outcomes will sit in the wider context. It will also put the understandable but rather insular 'What's in it for me?' approach into perspective. The partnership, as a single unit, will be able to explain its contribution; to suggest developments; to propose new partners; to action plan for further work or new directions. The ability to do this is an outcome of the successful blending of individual wish lists into a cohesive whole. This process means that individual partners may expect to be called on to contribute their time, their expertise, the resources of the organisations they represent including, on occasions, money. Fostering belief in the goals in common is one of the most critical challenges for the partnership manager. People will become individually committed only when there are clear benefits for them in being so.

Leadership

Partnerships need strong **leadership**. They operate on a level playing field where management is about applying inter-personal skills in order to build effective working relationships. This is part of the reason why impartial leadership is a favoured option and also why people steeped in the ethos of hierarchical organisations do not always make good partnership leaders and may make difficult partners. Managing a partnership is not about control, ownership and vested interest. It is not the same as leading an organisation. It is about creating and sustaining relationships and fostering a true spirit of cooperation. It is a facilitating and coordinating role that makes considerable demands on personal skills. Intuition, perceptiveness, conflict resolution, mediation, the ability to listen, to précis and to summarise will be essential. A good partnership leader will demonstrate commitment to the common aspirations of the partnership and the ability to piece together the demands and contributions of individuals in order that they serve the common good. In addition he or she must have sufficient understanding and knowledge of the context of the work to inspire confidence among other partners and to propose direction of travel and destination when necessary.

Bridging the gap between partnership and organisation

The role of partner makes demands on people that are likely to be different from those of the regular day job. **Partners** are charged with bridging the gap between what is decided strategically as a group and what happens on the ground within each organisation. They will also bring back to the partnership table the outcomes of work that takes place within their organisation and that contributes to the work of the partnership. This is a critical role if partnership is to avoid Huxham's 'collaborative inertia', a term that describes the partnership that exists but that fails to achieve anything.

Each partner will, like the partnership leader, have a broad understanding of the context of the partnership. He or she will bring specific strengths to the table to contribute to the partnership's goals and aspirations. Not every partner will have the same interests or skills. It will be the task of the partnership leader to map the mix of competences against the desired outcomes. It is neither likely nor necessary that all partners will be equal in their contribution. What is important is that the balance between input and reward is carefully managed so that partners understand from the outset what might be expected of them and what they, in turn, can expect to get out of being a partner.

Bridging the gap between partnership and organisation means that those involved in strategic groups, in particular, need to be in positions where they are empowered to act on behalf of the organisation unilaterally. Partnership can be adversely affected if partners are not able to make decisions and commitments on behalf of their organisations without referring everything back through internal management systems. It is crucial that the partner has an in-depth understanding of on-the-ground practice to avoid committing to something at partnership level that cannot realistically be achieved. This is a pertinent point within services that have limited management structures. It is all too easy to determine representation based on time available rather than expertise.

Partners must understand and sign up to the concept of collaboration. They will be required to balance the commitment and loyalty to an individual organisation that is a natural consequence of employment with commitment and loyalty to the achievement of the partnership goals. Partners need to be clear how the partnership will yield the 'what's in it for us' factor that organisations will expect. They may have to embrace compromise; wait for results; co-opt other members of their organisations to partnership actions; make the case for partnership within their organisation; change the way that work happens; sell their organisation's point of view to other partners. In short a host of actions that can be broadly described as brokerage.

The actions that contribute to being a successful partner are often more time consuming than the work demanded by the partnership. This fact is rarely acknowledged when partnerships are created, even more rarely funded and can subsume a disproportionate amount of each partner's contribution making the real outputs of partnership practice minimal.

Partners will be responsible for making sure that they fulfil their roles within the partnership. An obvious statement but a critical factor in success is that everyone pulls their weight. Collaboration carries with it the notion of cooperation. If a single member fails to carry out what has been agreed or is reluctant to fully commit to what the partnership has signed up for, there is a risk to the eventual outcome of the work and to the partnership's ability to carry on.

Sound business practice

We have seen that partnerships are frequently constrained by time. Smart partnerships operate from the start within an agreed business plan. This embraces sign-up from each partner to: communication strategies; attendance at meetings; roles within meetings; responsibilities outside meetings. It includes agreement about partnership documentation; about the chairing of meetings; the taking and circulation of minutes. As with any facet of partnership the business function must be negotiated and mutually agreeable to all partners. This is particularly pertinent within those partnerships that rely on the good will of individual partners to provide services such as minuting, for example, or where responsibility for partnership business rotates within the membership. Straightforward, simple business practice releases partner time and energy and means that the focus falls on the work and objectives of the collaboration.

Communication

One of the most important aspects of partnership practice is the issue of **communication**. The case studies demonstrate how effective partnerships thrive on common understanding and regular and efficient contact.

The fact that we do not all speak the same language is obvious in a European context but is a real issue for all partnerships that bring together diverse individuals and organisations. One fundamental principle of partnership practice is the right of partners to be kept informed, up-to-date and in touch with everything that is going on. That way there is no excuse for disengagement; everyone comes to meetings having had access to work that has happened in the interim; the project proceeds in a seamless fashion and does not lurch haphazardly from meeting to meeting.

There is a distinction to be made between the talking shop and the role of communication in partnership. The former is a sign of an unhealthy collaboration, the latter essential in successful partnership work.

The European partnerships show how investment in achieving a common understanding is time well spent. Partners must understand the views, concepts and cultures of others, how these relate to their own and to the partnership aspirations. There must be consensus about terminology and messages. Once any partner strays from his or her comfort zone and enters the world of another organisation the linguistic challenge is immediately clear. ALLEGRO's work in brokering alliances between education and social services show how much ground work must be undertaken to ensure that there is a good chance that people will be singing from the same hymn sheet.

The normal pattern of collaborative practice is regular, but not frequent, meetings with work plans in between. Most partners are taking partnership on within already hectic schedules. A sensitive communication strategy is one that regularly updates partners between meetings. Communication by email is the smartest and most effective way of achieving this. It enables the partnership leader to ensure that work is carried forward between face to face encounters. It enables partners to ask questions, raise issues, share outcomes, exchange news and views on a regular basis. This in turn saves time at meetings.

The conduct of partnership meetings must account for limited time and crowded agendas. Agreement about how information will be conveyed at meetings must be made early on. This might encompass the tabling of papers; formal reporting; a rota of longer presentations; informal debate; question and answer sessions. Whatever the process, each partner should be afforded time for his or her input. The management of this is a responsibility of the chair of the meeting.

Partners have a responsibility to communicate the work of the partnership within the organisations that they represent. This is essential to bond the work closely to the day-to-day functioning of the institution or service. The partnership, as part of a process of legitimisation, should also publicise its activity to the wider world. In doing so it will want to describe how the partnership operates as well as what has been achieved. A number of communication tools will help: partnership events; presence at meetings; regular inclusion on organisational agendas; specific partnership documentation (leaflets; newsletters; web page); contributions to conferences and workshops; links to local, regional and national networks.

A relatively informal way for organisations and partnerships involved in similar business to stay in contact with each other and to learn from each others' experiences is networking. Sometimes more formal partnership arrangements can arise from networking activity and networking is an integral feature of partnership practice. Adult educators are practised networkers and on local, regional and national levels there are examples of good networking practice supported by agencies such as CILT, the National Centre for Languages, ALL (the Association for Language Learning) and NIACE (the National Institute for Adult and Continuing Education).

Realistic goals

It is worth reiterating that partnership is the means by which commonly desired outcomes and **goals** are achieved. It is essentially a functional framework that frees people up to focus on the main purpose of working together. It would be unwise, however, to underestimate the time and energy necessary to bring a disparate group of individuals and organisations to the point where they operate as a single well-oiled machine. Setting realistic and achievable goals is essential to the well-being and longevity of any partnership. This may well mean that, at the outset, goals are short term and may not be in proportion to the combined talents and commitment of the partnership team. As the partnership grows in confidence more ambitious and wide ranging achievements may be sought. Success is essential to fuel the enthusiasm and allegiance of individual partners. Good planning will include both short- and longer term goals and aspirations and will articulate the partnership journey in steps that are measurable and that can be demonstrated. Every partnership must be able to explain clearly where it is going, how it intends to get there and the extent to which its objectives have been met. In this way the suspicions of the uncommitted can be allayed and the partnership itself generates momentum from being able to tick off successes.

Conclusion

We hope that this book has inspired you to either continue on your journey of collaborative working or, if you are a novice when it comes to collaboration, to give partnership working a go.

We have tried to show, through the case studies, different approaches to collaboration as well as areas where collaboration has proved successful. The list clearly does not claim to be exhaustive, as its compilation was informed by the authors' personal experiences – good, bad and frankly surprising! We aim to give a flavour, shot through with generic analysis, as well as personal experience in terms of pointers, pitfalls, etc.

At the heart of our commitment to collaboration was, and continues to be, a genuine curiosity about people and about how other people work. The reality of partnership working is sometimes frustrating, not a little challenging, often slow and arduous – yet learning from others is an immensely enriching experience.

This learning, which is enriching on a personal and a professional level, can take many forms. At its simplest, it is sometimes a realisation of how not to do something, which mistakes to avoid. Rather than staring at a blank page, somebody else's ideas, even if we do not agree with all of them, are a good starting point. Where someone's experience inspires replication, we can clearly save a lot of time and effort by short-circuiting the onerous learning curve that a partner may have experienced.

Successful collaboration often leads to further development and project work. In the Black Country, for example, following the end of the Pathfinder project, the proven success of working together led to the establishment of regional support structures around training and accreditation.

Partnerships, in the broadest sense of the word, are hard work – we did not intend to gloss over this self-evident fact. There are moments when we think, 'If we had done this ourselves, it would have gone much more smoothly.' However, where collaboration is more than lip service, it is personally and professionally re-invigorating. In the context of adult education language learning and teaching it benefits teachers, organisations, whole areas and, most significantly, enriches the language learning experience for our learners – and long may it continue!

So you think partnership working is for you?

What makes a good partnership?

❑ Clear leadership

❑ A purpose that is in accord with mine

❑ A varied group of people who bring different strengths and perspectives to it

❑ Well-motivated participants

❑ Evidence that positive outcomes are on the cards

❑ Good management and work planning

❑ A sound reputation

What makes a good partnership leader?

❑ Impartiality

❑ Strong interpersonal skills

❑ Empathy with the cause of the partnership

❑ Ability to manage through consensus and compromise

❑ Good networks and networking

❑ Enthusiasm, drive and energy

What makes a good partner?

❑ Commitment and co-operation

❑ Ability to see more than one side of the story

❑ Skills of brokerage

❑ Ability to compromise

❑ Strengths and skills that support the aims of the partnership

❑ The right person from an organisation, not the person with the most time

❑ Motivated to work in collaboration

❑ Ability to relate personal objectives to the goals of the partnership

What are good outcomes?

☐ The solution of a problem in common

☐ Financial benefits

☐ The development of new ideas and new work

☐ The co-option of new learners

☐ The improvement of quality

☐ Keeping in touch with and responding to change

☐ Looking at languages from different perspectives

☐ Creating different opportunities for language learning

☐ Networking

☐ Not working in isolation

☐ Challenging moribund practice

☐ Smart and relevant language programmes

Bibliography

Atkinson, M., Wilkin. A., Stott, A., Doherty, P. and Kinder, K. (2002) *Multi-agency working: A detailed study* (LGA Research Report 26). NFER.

Audit Commission (1998) *A fruitful partnership: Effective partnership working*. Audit Commission.

Fletcher-Campbell, F. (1997) *The education of children who are looked after*. NFER.

Gilbert, I. (2002) *Essential motivation in the classroom*. RoutledgeFarmer.

Hargreaves, D. (2003) *Education epidemic: Transforming secondary schools through innovation networks*. DEMOS.

Haynes, J., Atkinson, M. and Kinder, K. (1999) *Starting to join: A baseline study of multi-agency activity for north east Lincolnshire LEA*. NFER.

Johnstone, D. (2003) *Partnerships: Benefits, limitations and doing it better*. Learning and Skills Development Agency.

Kennedy, H. (1997) *Learning works: Widening participation in further education* (Kennedy Report). FEFC.

Lumby, J. and Foskett, N. (2005) *14-19 education: Policy, leadership and learning*. Sage Publications.

The Nuffield Languages Inquiry (2000) *Languages: The next generation*. The Nuffield Foundation.

OdLL project partners (2005) *Opening the door to language learning: Bringing language learning to the wider community*. Drukkenij De Beurs.

Tomlinson, K. (2003) *Effective inter-agency working: a review of literature and examples from practice*. NFER.

Watters, K. (2005) *More than the sum: Partnerships for adult learning and skills*. NIACE.